UKULELE

YESTERDAY

MUSIC FROM THE ORIGINAL MOTION PICTURE SOUNDTRACK

© 2019 UNIVERSAL STUDIOS

ISBN 978-1-5400-6433-2

Visit Hal Leonard Online at
www.halleonard.com

Contact us:
Hal Leonard
7777 West Bluemound Road
Milwaukee, WI 53213
Email: info@halleonard.com

In Europe, contact:
Hal Leonard Europe Limited
42 Wigmore Street
Marylebone, London, W1U 2RN
Email: info@halleonardeurope.com

In Australia, contact:
Hal Leonard Australia Pty. Ltd.
4 Lentara Court
Cheltenham, Victoria, 3192 Australia
Email: info@halleonard.com.au

All You Need Is Love

Words and Music by John Lennon and Paul McCartney

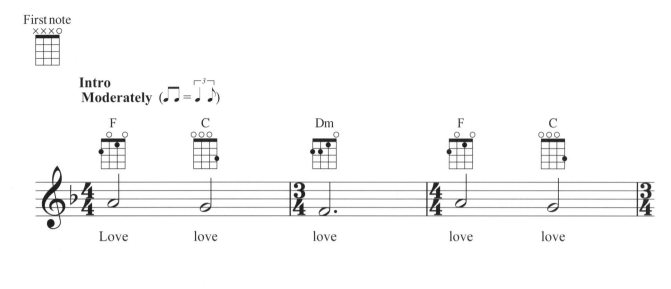

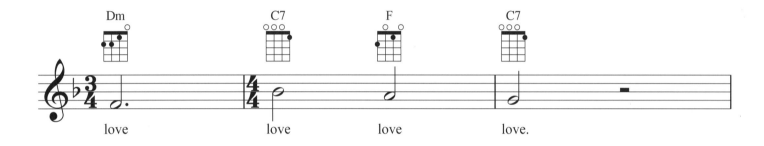

Love   love   love   love   love

love   love   love   love.

(Instrumental)

1. There's noth-ing you can do   that   can't be   done. ____
2. There's noth-ing you can make   that   can't be   made. ____
3. There's noth-ing you can know   that   is - n't   known. ____

Love is all _____ you need.

Outro-Chorus

Coda

All you need is love. _____ (All to - geth - er now.) _

All you need is love. _____ (Ev -'ry - bod - y.) All you need is love, _

_____ love. _____ Love is all _ you need.

Love is all _____ you need.

Back in the U.S.S.R.

Words and Music by John Lennon and Paul McCartney

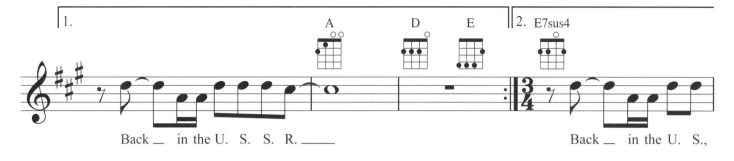

Back — in the U. S. S. R. ——   Back — in the U. S.,

back — in the U. S.,   back — in the U. S. S. R. ——   Well, the

Bridge

U - kraine girls real - ly knock me out. — They leave — the — West be - hind. —

—   And Mos - cow girls make me sing and shout — that

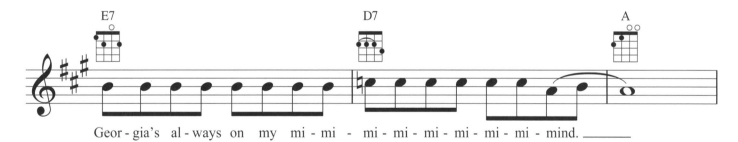

Geor - gia's al - ways on my mi - mi - mi - mi - mi - mi - mi - mi - mind. ——

D.C. al Coda

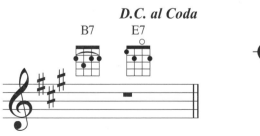

Back — in the U. S. S. R. ——

Carry That Weight

Words and Music by John Lennon and Paul McCartney

Verse

I nev - er give you my pil - low, ___

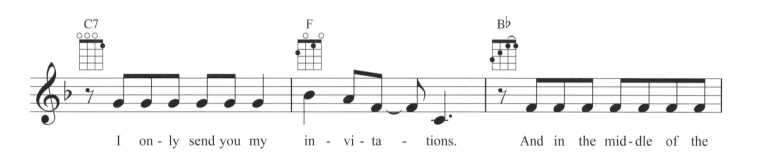

I on - ly send you my in - vi - ta - tions. And in the mid - dle of the

D.C. al Coda

cel - e - bra - tions, I break down. ___

Coda

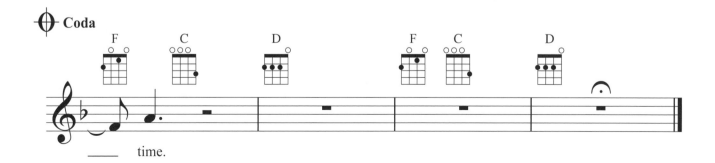

___ time.

A Hard Day's Night

Words and Music by John Lennon and Paul McCartney

work - ing _____ like a dog. _____ It's been a hard day's night. _
mon - ey _____ to buy you things. _____ And it's worth it just to hear you say _

_____ I should be sleep - ing _____ like a log. _____ But when I
_____ you're gon - na give me _____ ev - 'ry - thing. _____ So why I

get home to you, _____ I find the things that you do _____ will make me
love to come home, _ 'cause when I get you a - lone, _____ you know I'll

Help!

Words and Music by John Lennon and Paul McCartney

days are gone, _ I'm not so self - as - sured; _____ now I find I've
now and then, _ I feel so in - se - cure, _____ I know that I just

Chorus

changed my mind. I've o - pened up the doors. _⎱ Help me if you
need you like I've nev - er done be - fore. _⎰

can, I'm feel - ing down. _____ And I do _____ ap - pre - ci - ate _

_____ you be - ing 'round. _____ Help me get _ my feet _

_____ back on the ground, _____ won't you please, please _ help _ me? _

1., 2. ‖ 3.

_____ Help me, help me. _____ Ooh.

15

Hey Jude

Words and Music by John Lennon and Paul McCartney

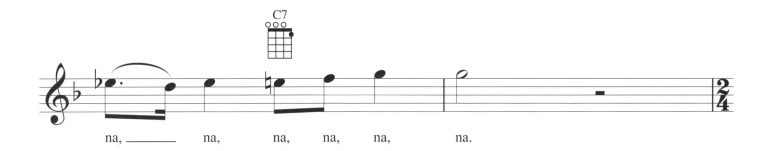

na, _____ na, na, na, na, na.

Verse

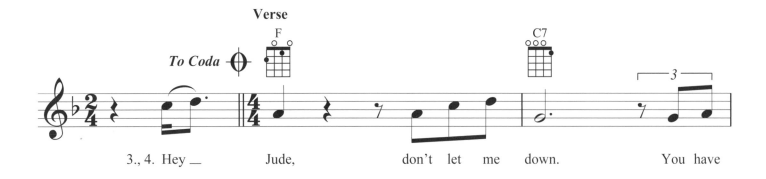

3., 4. Hey __ Jude, don't let me down. You have

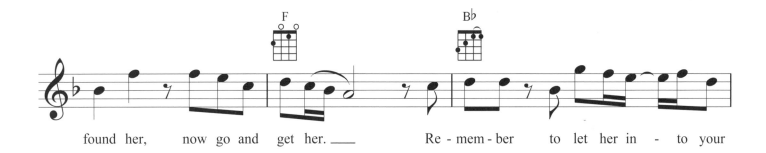

found her, now go and get her. ___ Re - mem - ber to let her in - to your

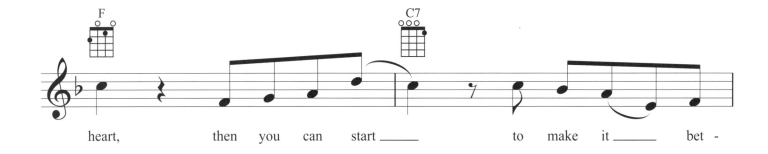

heart, then you can start _____ to make it _____ bet -

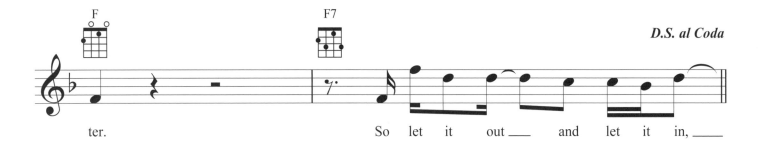

D.S. al Coda

ter. So let it out ___ and let it in, ___

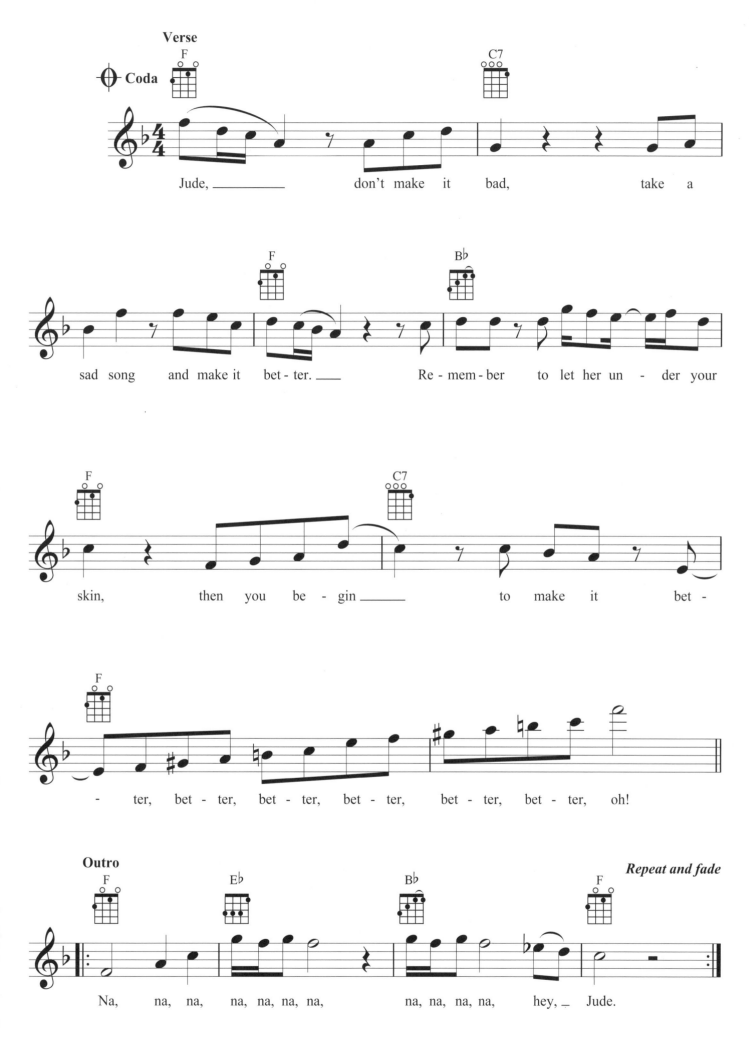

I Saw Her Standing There

Words and Music by John Lennon and Paul McCartney

Chorus

how could I dance with an - oth - er, _____
She would - n't dance with an - oth - er, _____

oh, when I saw her stand - ing
oh, when I saw her stand - ing

1. there?   2. Well,

2. there.

Bridge

Well, my heart went

boom when I crossed that room and I held her

hand in mine. _____   3. Well, we

21

Verse

danced through the night ___ and we held each oth - er tight, ___

___ and be - fore too long, ___ I fell in love with

her. _____ Now, I'll nev - er

dance with an - oth - er, _____ oh, since I

saw her stand - ing there. _____

Here Comes the Sun

Words and Music by George Harrison

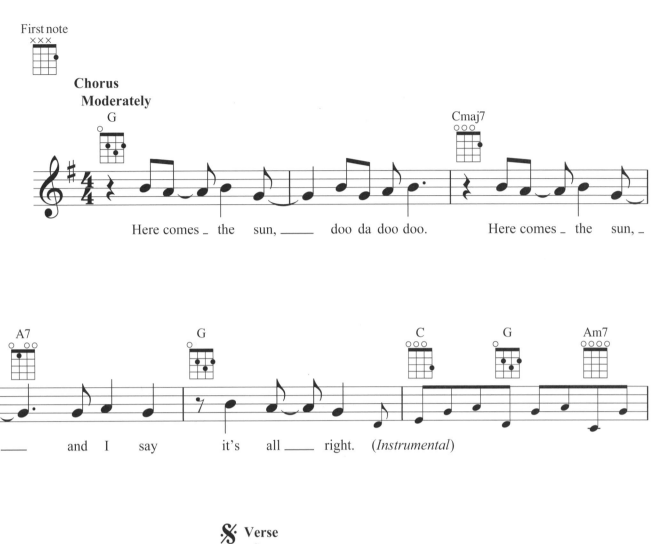

Here comes _ the sun, _____ doo da doo doo. Here comes _ the sun, _

_____ and I say it's all _____ right. (*Instrumental*)

1. Lit - tle dar - ling,   it's been _ a long, _
2. Lit - tle dar - ling,   the smiles _ re - turn -
3. Lit - tle dar - ling,   I feel _ that ice _

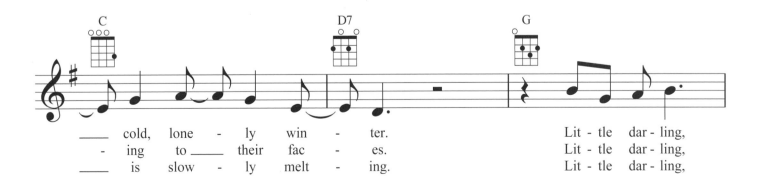

_____ cold, lone - ly win - ter.   Lit - tle dar - ling,
- ing to _ their fac - es.   Lit - tle dar - ling,
_____ is slow - ly melt - ing.   Lit - tle dar - ling,

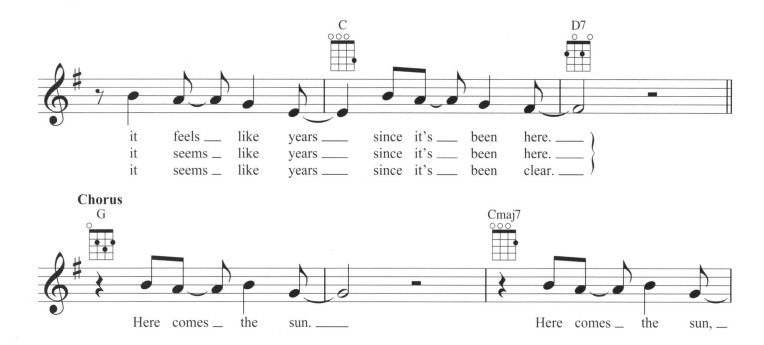

it feels _ like years _ since it's _ been here. __
it seems _ like years _ since it's _ been here. __
it seems _ like years _ since it's _ been clear. __

Chorus

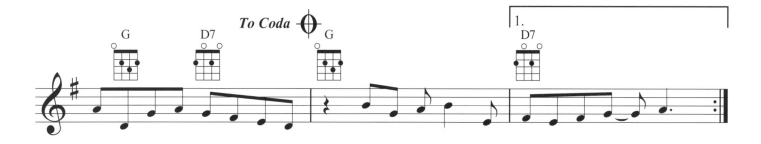

Here comes _ the sun. ____ Here comes _ the sun, _

__ and I say it's all _ right. (*Instrumental*)

To Coda

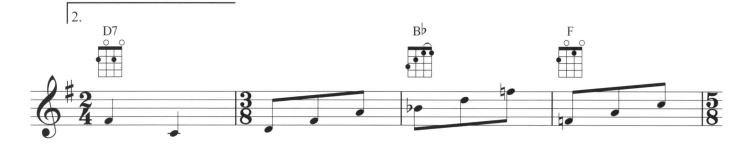

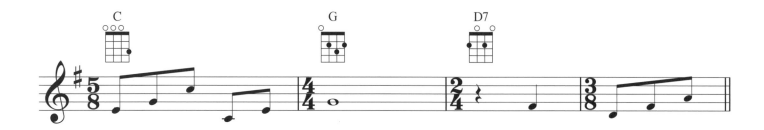

Sun, sun, sun, here it comes. (*Instrumental*)

(*Instrumental*)

Here comes __ the sun. ____ Here comes __ the sun, __

__ it's all __ right. (*Instrumental*)

It's all __ right. (*Instrumental*)

In My Life

Words and Music by John Lennon and Paul McCartney

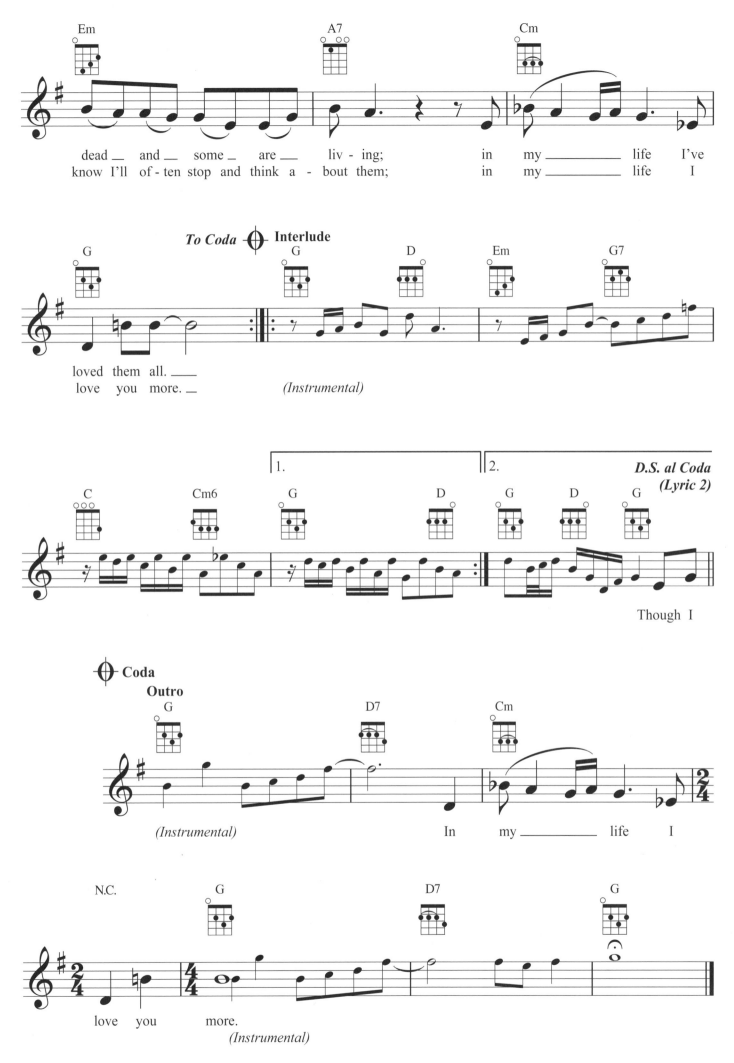

dead _ and _ some _ are _ liv - ing;   in   my _____ life   I've
know I'll of - ten stop and think a - bout them;   in   my _____ life   I

To Coda **Interlude**

loved them all. ____
love you more. ____   *(Instrumental)*

1.   2.   ***D.S. al Coda***
(Lyric 2)

Though I

Coda
Outro

(Instrumental)   In   my _____ life   I

N.C.

love you   more.
(Instrumental)

27

Let It Be

Words and Music by John Lennon and Paul McCartney

be. ——————

be. ——————

Chorus

Let it be, ———— let it be, ———— let it be, —

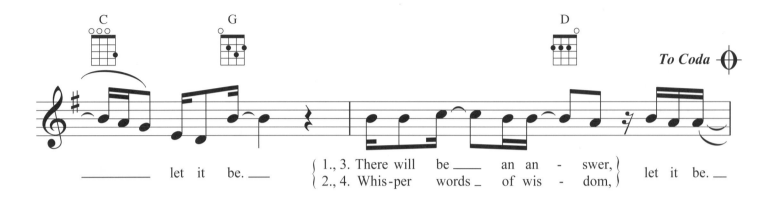

To Coda ⊕

———— let it be. —

{ 1., 3. There will be —— an an - swer, }
{ 2., 4. Whis - per words — of wis - dom, }

let it be. —

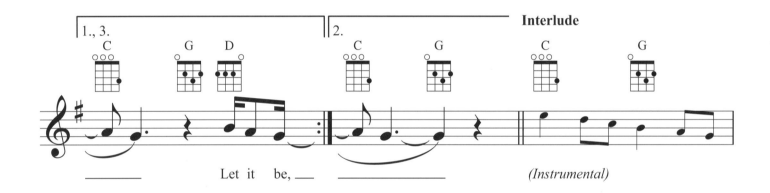

Interlude

1., 3.

2.

———— Let it be, — ————————

(Instrumental)

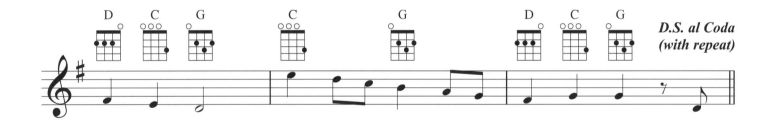

D.S. al Coda
(with repeat)

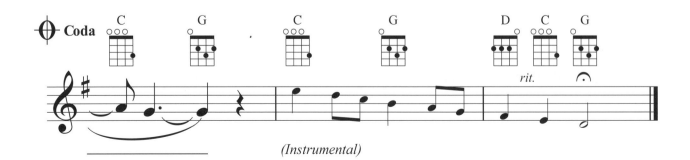

⊕ **Coda**

rit.

———————— *(Instrumental)*

I Want to Hold Your Hand

Words and Music by John Lennon and Paul McCartney

The Long and Winding Road

Words and Music by John Lennon and Paul McCartney

man - y times __ I've cried. __ An - y - way, __ you'll nev - er know __ the

Verse

man - y ways __ I've tried. __ And/But } still they lead me back ____ to the long __

Instrumental ends

____ wind - ing road. ____ You left me stand - ing here

a long, long time a - go. ____ Don't { leave / keep } me wait -

To Coda ✛

D.S. al Coda

- ing here. Lead me to your __ door.

✛ **Coda**

door. Yeah, yeah, yeah, yeah. ____

She Loves You

Words and Music by John Lennon and Paul McCartney

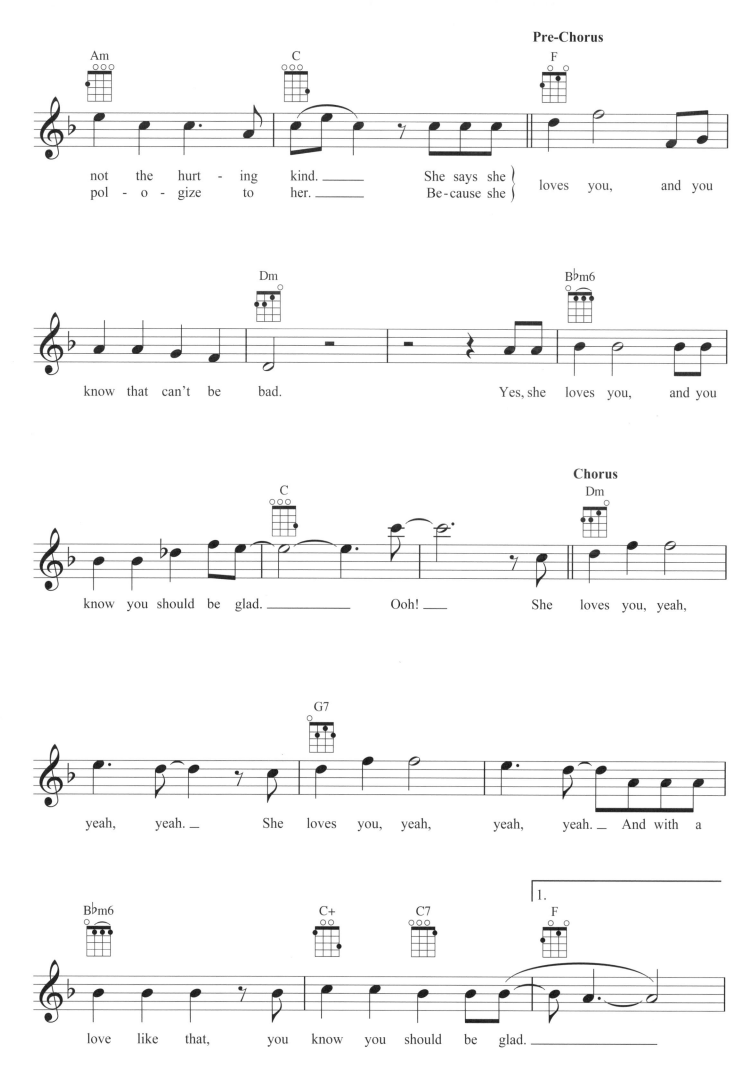

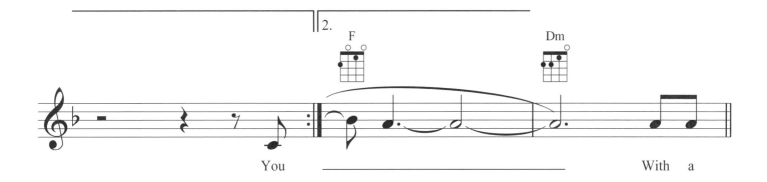

You _____ With a

Outro

love like that, you know you should be glad. _____

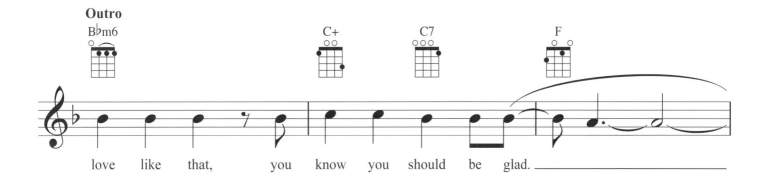

_____ With a love like that, you know you should _____ be

glad. Yeah, yeah, yeah, _____ yeah,

yeah, yeah, _____ yeah, yeah, yeah, yeah!

Something

Words and Music by George Harrison

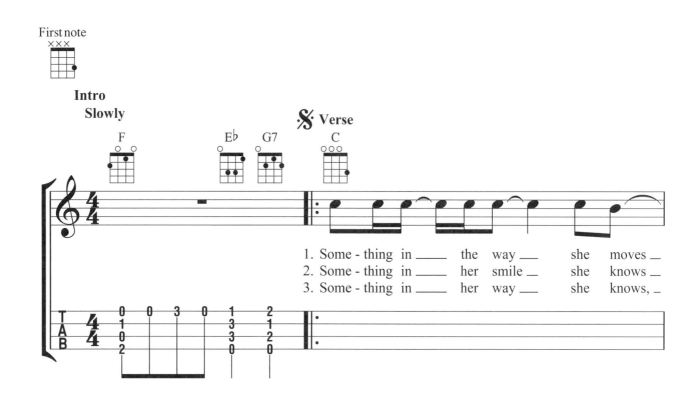

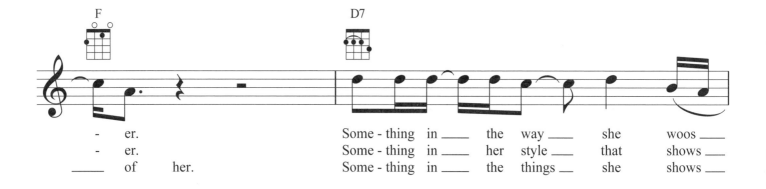

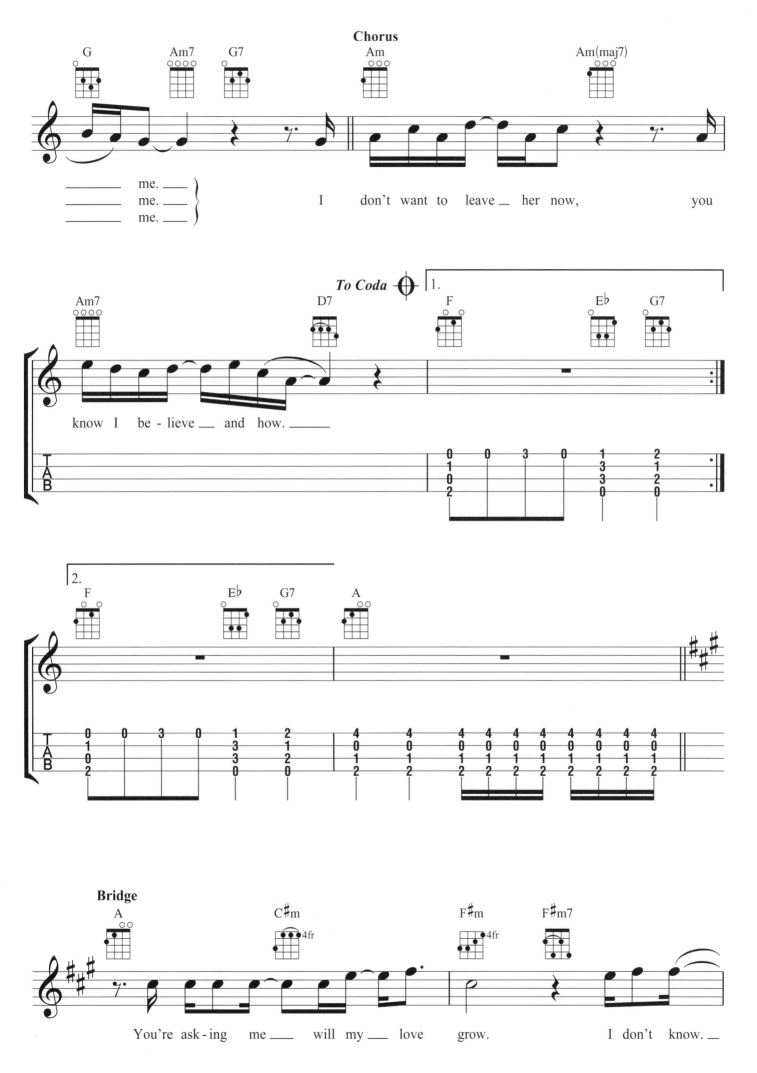

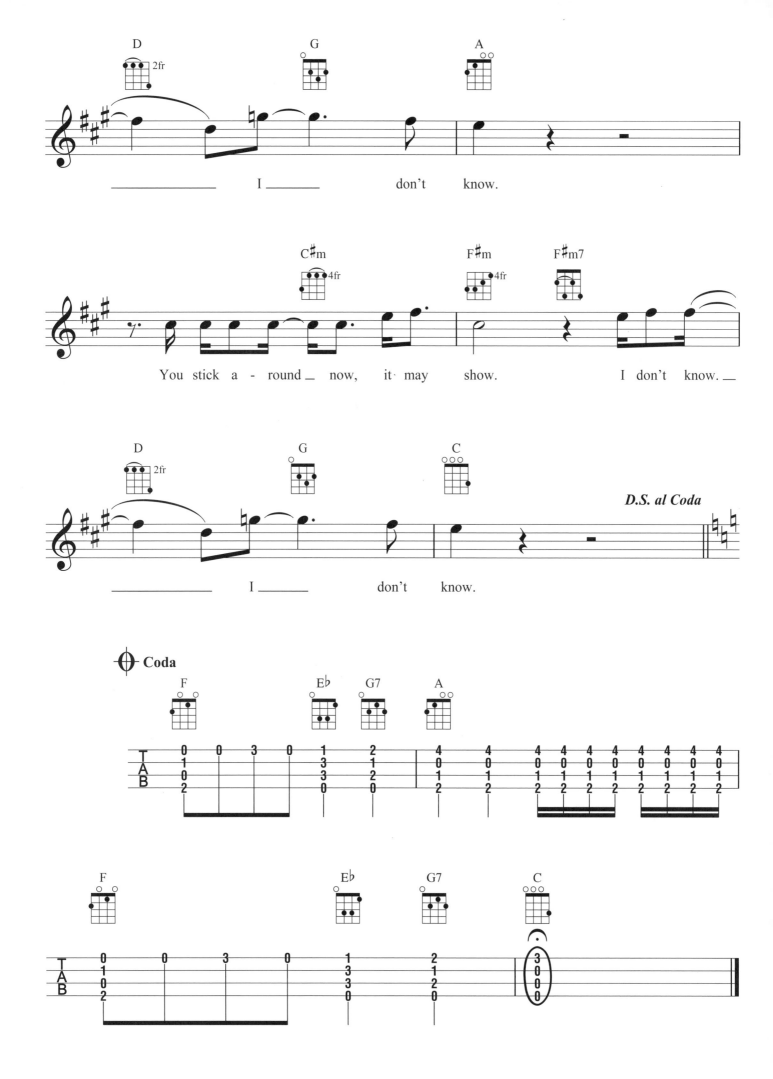

Chorus
G Am7 G7 Am Am(maj7)
me.
me.
me.
I don't want to leave her now, you
To Coda
1.
Am7 D7 F E♭ G7
know I be - lieve and how.
2.
F E♭ G7 A
Bridge
A C♯m F♯m F♯m7
4fr
4fr
You're ask - ing me will my love grow. I don't know.

Ob-La-Di, Ob-La-Da

Words and Music by John Lennon and Paul McCartney

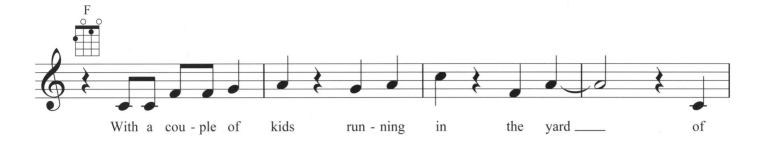

With a cou - ple of kids run - ning in the yard _____ of

1st time, D.C.
2nd time, D.C. al Coda

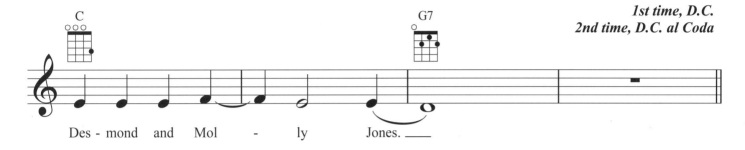

Des - mond and Mol - ly Jones. _____

Coda

_____ And if you want some fun, _____

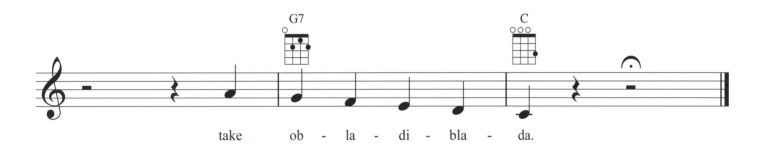

take ob - la - di - bla - da.

Additional Lyrics

2. Desmond takes a trolley to the jeweler's store,
   Buys a twenty-carat golden ring.
   Takes it back to Molly waiting at the door,
   And as he gives it to her she begins to sing:

3. Happy ever after in the marketplace,
   Desmond lets the children lend a hand.
   Molly stays at home and does her pretty face,
   And in the evening she still sings it with the band.

4. Happy ever after in the marketplace,
   Molly lets the children lend a hand.
   Desmond stays at home and does his pretty face,
   And in the evening she's a singer with the band.

Yesterday

Words and Music by John Lennon and Paul McCartney

know, she would - n't say. _____ I said

some - thing wrong, now I long for yes - ter - day. _____

Verse

3., 4. Yes - ter - day, ___ love was such an eas - y

game to play. ___ Now I need a place to

hide a - way. ___ Oh, I be - lieve _____ in

Outro

yes - ter - day. ___ Mm, _____ mm, mm, mm. ___